英語長文問題

CROSSOVER

2

Daiichi Gakushusha

本書の使い方
HOW TO USE CROSSOVER

本文の語数と, 本文を読むための目標時間です。

すべての問題を解くための制限時間です。

本文に関連する教科やSDGsを示します。英文を読む力に加え, 他の教科等や社会の諸問題に関する知見を深める問題集です。

Lesson 3

語数(速読目標時間)	関連教科	関連SDGs	得点
322(3分15秒)	公民		/ 50
制限時間 20分			

レッスンは難易度順に配列しました。
CROSSOVER ②では
350〜500語の英文を
中心に収録しています。

英文の選定基準
・他の教科等で学習する内容を含むもの
・SDGsの17の目標に深く関連したもの
・現代的な話題

CROSSOVER ②では
CEFR-A2レベルを
到達目標に設定し,
本文は**CEFR-A2レベル**
の文法で
構成しました。

脚注の二次元コードから, 本文の音声を聞くことができます。
・情報料は無料ですが, 通信費は利用者の負担となります。
・本書の発行終了とともに上記コンテンツの配信を終了することがあります。

英文を読みやすくするため, 脚注では語の注釈を多めに取り上げています。覚えるべき語句として, 別冊『多読と整理』で同じ語句を取り上げている場合もあります。

1 The number of foreign workers in Japan is increasing. According to the Ministry of Health, Labor and Welfare (MHLW), the number was nearly 1.3 million in 2018. The government's policy is to accept more foreign workers in order to *ease labor shortages. In fact, (1)a new visa status was created in April 2019. The status allows a
5 maximum five-year *residency to foreigners who have specific skills in 14 industries including nursing and food service. The new status provides the labor market with another 345,000 foreign workers over a five-year period.

2 MHLW also reported that in 2018, 20 percent of foreign workers were (2)technical interns. They came to Japan to learn specific skills under a national training program.
10 The program aims to contribute to developing countries by transferring job skills. These skills include manufacturing foods and clothes, and constructing buildings. The interns come from countries such as Vietnam, China, the Philippines, and Indonesia. They are allowed to stay in Japan for up to five years. Some employers in the agricultural and fishery *sectors say that their businesses might fail without access to
15 such workers.

3 Nowadays, accepting more foreign workers for a longer time span is under debate. If technical interns get the new status after acquiring a specific skill, they can be permitted to stay for up to 10 years. However, Professor Kiyoto Tanno of Tokyo Metropolitan University says that this is still rather short. He warns that as long as
20 they are considered *temporary workers, the skills they can learn are limited. Thus, many foreign workers will continue to fill the shortages of low-*wage workers. Actually, the poor working conditions for interns, such as low wages, long working hours, and poor safety measures [...] should allow [...] (3)Otherwis [...]

ease：…を緩和する　　residency：居住, 在留　　sector：分野　　temporary：一時的な　　wage：賃金

別冊『多読と整理』の使い方
HOW TO USE THE ANNEX

■多読
別冊は見開き構成で, 左ページは
「本文と同じテーマの別英文とその設問」で構成しています。
メール・広告・記事など, さまざまなテキストタイプの英文を読むことができます。
本文を読む前の背景知識の習得や,
本文を読んだ後の追加演習として使うことができます。

設問に解答するために必要な力を「タグ」として示しました。

📝 **知識・技能**：語彙・文法・句読法などに関わる問題です。

📝 **主題**：文章全体や段落の主題を把握する問題です。速読スキルを身に付けることができます。

📝 **文章展開**：段落どうしのつながりに関わる問題です。

📝 **段落構成**：一つの段落の構成などに関わる問題です。パラグラフ・ライティングの参考にすることもできます。

📝 **論理**：ディスコースマーカーなどの文脈や，どうしてそう言えるのかを問う問題です。

※その他，問題に応じたタグを付けています。

---

1. According to (1)a new visa status, who is most likely to stay in Japan till 2026? 📝 **内容理解** (7点)

a. Jasmin
Nationality : the Philippines
Date of visa renewal :
Sep. 22, 2022
Career :
Worked as a nurse for 5 years

b. Nguyen
Nationality : Vietnam
Date of visa renewal :
April 30, 2019
Career :
Managed a shrimp farm from childhood

c. Sari
Nationality : Indonesia
Date of visa renewal :
Mar. 3, 2022
Career :
None (Just graduated from high school)

d. Zhang
Nationality : China
Date of visa renewal :
May 31, 2020
Career :
Constructed schools in rural areas

2. (2)Technical interns _____. 📝 **主題** (7点)

a. account for the majority of foreign workers
b. can stay in Japan for more than 10 years if they want
c. come to Japan to provide specific technical skills
d. work in the agricultural and fishery sectors in Japan

3. If you agree with Prof. Kiyoto Tanno's opinion, which statement best expresses your view? 📝 **主張の意図** (8点)

a. Chances to learn more specialized skills should be given to foreign workers.
b. If technical interns are willing to work in several industrial sectors, they should stay longer.
c. It is important for foreign workers to learn fundamental skills first.

設問文は英語で記されています。

よく使われる表現を確認しておきましょう。

According to the text [passage], ...「本文によると，…。」
→本文にない内容を答えないようにしましょう。

Be sure to make ... clear.「…を明確にしなさい。」
→…には指示表現などが入ります。指示表現の内容を明確にして答えましょう。

Explain in detail ....「詳しく説明しなさい。」
→支持文の内容なども交えて，できるだけ詳細に答えましょう。

Translate the following into Japanese: ....「…以下を日本語に翻訳しなさい。」
→なるべく自然な日本語になるよう心がけましょう。

You may choose more than one option.「選択肢を二つ以上選んでもよい。」
→複数解答が正答になる可能性があります。

設問の工夫

・選択式と記述式のバランスに留意しました。
　※記述式は日本語記述が中心です。

・筆者の意図や，「なぜこの語を使ったか」を問う問題を採用しました。
　※モデルとなる本文を多く読むことで，「書く」技能を向上させることもできます。

・本文と日常生活をリンクさせて解答する問題を採用しました。

・選択式では，消去法が最適の解法となる問題を可能なかぎり避けました。

・文法的な正しさや，用語や用法の区別が中心となる問題を避けました。

・和訳問題や，該当箇所を和訳することで答える問題を少なくしました。
　※ 📝 **知識・技能** タグの問題は和訳問題が中心です。

「解答・解説集」で，選択式の「誤りの選択肢」の根拠や，記述式の「答案例と採点基準」などを示しています。

■整理

右ページは「本文の設問の解答欄」「語句の意味調べ」「要約完成」で構成しています。

本文の設問の解答欄

語句の意味調べ：意味を知っておくべき単語をピックアップしました。取り上げられた単語や表現の意味を書いて覚えましょう（本文の脚注で同じ語句を扱っている場合があります）。

要約完成：本文の概要を理解できたか，要約完成で確認しましょう。ここでは空所補充形式としていますが，慣れてきたら自分で本文を要約し，ストーリーリテリングにも挑戦してみましょう。

CONTENTS

語数(速読目標時間)	関連教科	関連SDGs	得 点
340(3分25秒)			
制限時間	外国語	—	
20分			/ 50

1 Every day, a *vast number of airplanes fly in the skies around the world. They travel through the airways and land at airports without colliding with each other. (1)How is it possible for airplanes to fly so safely?

2 To ensure that airplanes arrive at their destinations safely and efficiently, air traffic
5 controllers instruct pilots on *altitude, speed, and direction over the radio. They are the *commanders of the sky. As a general rule, they use only English when they communicate with pilots over the radio, *regardless of the pilot's nationality. This is because if air traffic controllers give instructions freely in their own language, they cannot communicate well with pilots from other countries. English is (2)the official
10 language of the "sky."

3 However, (3)the English spoken by pilots and air traffic controllers is far from the English we all speak in our daily lives. It's so different, in fact, that even the most fluent native English speakers need training to understand it. This unique language of the sky is called "*Aviation English." It includes a specialized alphabet and vocabulary
15 *consisting of about 300 aviation terms.

4 For example, pilots and air traffic controllers do not use the words "Yes" or "No." Instead, they use the word "Affirm" when they agree with or approve of something. On the other hand, to deny, they use the word "Negative" instead of "No." The words "Yes" and "No" are too short and may not be heard, so longer words are used to avoid
20 misunderstandings.

5 This unique use of English is also seen when pilots and air traffic controllers say certain numbers. The letters " 3," " 5," and " 9" are read as "tree," "fife," and "niner" *respectively. This pronunciation rule is called (4)the "Phonetic Code," a reading system unique to Aviation English. It was created to make it easier for non-native English
25 speakers to pronounce those words. In the Phonetic Code, alphabetic letters are also read differently from the general alphabet. The letter "A" is pronounced as "Alpha," so when saying "A 9," it is pronounced as "Alpha, Niner."

---

vast：膨大な　　altitude：高度　　commander：司令官，指揮官　　regardless of ... : …に関係なく　　aviation：航空
consist of ... : …で構成されている　　respectively：それぞれ

本文音声

1. (1)How is it possible for airplanes to fly so safely? Explain in Japanese. ⤷ 主題 (9点)

_____

_____

2. According to the paragraph 2, why did English become (2)the official language of the "sky"?
Explain in Japanese. ⤷ 抽象と具体 (9点)

_____

_____

3. Translate the following into Japanese: (3)the English spoken by pilots and air traffic
controllers is far from the English we all speak in our daily lives. ⤷ 知識・技能 (9点)

_____

_____

4. Regarding (4)the "Phonetic Code," we can say [_____]. ⤷ キーワードの理解 (7点)
　　a. a fluent native English speaker can understand it without difficulty
　　b. many non-native English speakers find that [θ] and [v] are hard to pronounce
　　c. more and more English learners pronounce "A" as "Alpha"
　　d. there are some numbers whose sounds are similar and confusing

5. Which of the following statements is true? ⤷ 内容理解 (7点)
　　a. Air traffic controllers want to use shorter words in order to communicate quickly.
　　b. Aviation English refers to special pronunciations of alphabet letters and numbers.
　　c. Pilots and air traffic controllers are supposed to use English when they
　　　communicate.
　　d. Pilots are often regarded as the commanders of the sky.

6. Why was "Aviation English" created as a communication tool between pilots and air traffic
controllers instead of ordinary English? Explain in Japanese. ⤷ 要約 (9点)

_____

_____

語数(速読目標時間)	関連教科	関連 SDGs	得 点
372(3分40秒)	情報	—	
制限時間			
20分			/ 50

1 Social media are important tools in our daily lives today. They make our lives very exciting. How do you use these useful tools? Do you post pictures of yourself and your friends? Do you introduce your favorite video clips or photos? Or, do you post your opinions about some social problems? If you have done any of these things, you
5 have left (1)a "digital tattoo" on the Internet.

2 Information once published on the web, such as posts and photos, is easily copied and stored. Therefore, even if you delete the information from your social media or blogs, somebody else may have saved it and spread it. In other words, you cannot completely delete it once you've posted it. "Once-spread information" will remain
10 forever as long as there is the Internet in the world. It is like a "tattoo" that is difficult to erase once this is put in.

3 Digital tattoos can be very damaging to a person's life. For example, when you take an entrance examination or hunt for a job, your name could be searched on the web. If some problems you have caused in the past are found, you might be refused
15 *admission or employment. For people who don't know you well, the content written there is the only thing that explains you. You won't be able to *get rid of the label, "you're a problematic person." This is why digital tattoos are so troublesome. They may continue to *ruin your life. What is worse, they can harm people around you such as your parents and friends.

20 **4** There (2)used to be a saying "*A wonder lasts but nine days." However, in today's digital society, a *gossip may last ninety years or more. (3)As social media become more and more popular, the problem of digital tattoos is becoming more and more serious. Then, what can we do to avoid leaving damaging digital tattoos? First, do not post personal information, such as your name, pictures, address and so on, on the
25 Internet. Second, be careful what you say on social media. You must not post anything that will hurt other people. It is true that social media are really convenient tools, but we need to rethink how to get along with them.

---

admission：入学　　get rid of ...：…を取り除く　　ruin：…を破滅させる
A wonder lasts but nine days.：人の噂も七十五日(ことわざ)　　gossip：(よくない)噂[ゴシップ]

　本文音声

1. Why is something which you posted on the web called (1)a "digital tattoo"? Explain in Japanese. ⤷ 論理 (7点)

_____

_____

2. What damage can digital tattoos do to a person's life? Explain in Japanese. ⤷ 論理 (7点)

_____

_____

3. The writer used (2)used to in order to ☐. ⤷ 知識・技能 (7点)
   a. say that people tend to use the saying in many situations
   b. show that the saying is not in use anymore
   c. suggest that the saying is not correct in some situations today
   d. tell us that many people have used the saying in their speeches, etc

4. Translate the following into Japanese: (3)As social media become more and more popular, the problem of digital tattoos is becoming more and more serious. ⤷ 知識・技能 (7点)

_____

_____

5. In order not to leave damaging digital tattoos, what can we do? Explain in Japanese. ⤷ 段落構成 (各4点)

   • _____

   • _____

6. The writer thinks that ☐. ⤷ 筆者の意見 (7点)
   a. although social media are convenient tools, we need to be careful about how we use them
   b. digital tattoos should be as stylish as real tattoos
   c. not all digital tattoos are harmful; sometimes they benefit us
   d. we should stop using social media to avoid leaving digital tattoos

7. Which post is most unlikely to leave damaging digital tattoos? ⤷ まとめの段落 (7点)
   a. Game Blog ─ I Finally Completed *Dragon Hunter 12*
   b. The Player XXXX Shouldn't Be Listed on the National Soccer Team
   c. (With a clip) With My Best Friend Ayaka @Hakone
   d. (With a picture) Enjoyed a BBQ in My Yard #BBQ

Lesson 3

語数（速読目標時間）	関連教科	関連SDGs	得 点
322（3分15秒）	公民	8 DECENT WORK AND ECONOMIC GROWTH　17 PARTNERSHIPS FOR THE GOALS	/ 50
制限時間 20分			

1 The number of foreign workers in Japan is increasing. According to the Ministry of Health, Labor and Welfare (MHLW), the number was nearly 1.3 million in 2018. The government's policy is to accept more foreign workers in order to *ease labor shortages. In fact, (1)a new visa status was created in April 2019. The status allows a
5　maximum five-year *residency to foreigners who have specific skills in 14 industries including nursing and food service. The new status provides the labor market with another 345,000 foreign workers over a five-year period.

2 MHLW also reported that in 2018, 20 percent of foreign workers were (2)technical interns. They came to Japan to learn specific skills under a national training program.
10　The program aims to contribute to developing countries by transferring job skills. These skills include manufacturing foods and clothes, and constructing buildings. The interns come from countries such as Vietnam, China, the Philippines, and Indonesia. They are allowed to stay in Japan for up to five years. Some employers in the agricultural and fishery *sectors say that their businesses might fail without access to
15　such workers.

3 Nowadays, accepting more foreign workers for a longer time span is under debate. If technical interns get the new status after acquiring a specific skill, they can be permitted to stay for up to 10 years. However, Professor Kiyoto Tanno of Tokyo Metropolitan University says that this is still rather short. He warns that as long as
20　they are considered *temporary workers, the skills they can learn are limited. Thus, many foreign workers will continue to fill the shortages of low-*wage workers. Actually, the poor working conditions for interns, such as low wages, long working hours, and poor safety measures have already become a serious problem. Tanno suggests that Japan should allow foreign workers to stay longer so that they can learn
25　more advanced skills. (3)Otherwise, in the future, they may no longer choose Japan as a work destination.

---

ease：…を緩和する　　residency：居住，在留　　sector：分野　　temporary：一時的な　　wage：賃金

本文音声

1. According to (1)a new visa status, who is most likely to stay in Japan till 2026? ⟲内容理解 (7点)

a. Jasmin
Nationality : the Philippines
Date of visa renewal :
  Sep. 22, 2022
Career :
  Worked as a nurse for
  5 years

b. Nguyen
Nationality : Vietnam
Date of visa renewal :
  April 30, 2019
Career :
  Managed a shrimp farm
  from childhood

c. Sari
Nationality : Indonesia
Date of visa renewal :
  Mar. 3, 2022
Career :
  None (Just graduated
  from high school)

d. Zhang
Nationality : China
Date of visa renewal :
  May 31, 2020
Career :
  Constructed schools in
  rural areas

2. (2)Technical interns ☐. ⟲主題 (7点)
  a. account for the majority of foreign workers
  b. can stay in Japan for more than 10 years if they want
  c. come to Japan to provide specific technical skills
  d. work in the agricultural and fishery sectors in Japan

3. If you agree with Prof. Kiyoto Tanno's opinion, which statement best expresses your view?
  ⟲主張の意図 (8点)
  a. Chances to learn more specialized skills should be given to foreign workers.
  b. If technical interns are willing to work in several industrial sectors, they should
    stay longer.
  c. It is important for foreign workers to learn fundamental skills first.
  d. The government should stop extending visas unless foreign workers get a specific skill.

4. Translate the following into Japanese: (3)Otherwise, in the future, they may no longer choose
  Japan as a work destination. Be sure to make "Otherwise" and "they" clear. ⟲知識・技能 (10点)

_____

_____

5. Why does the writer think there is a problem with the system of accepting foreign workers?
  Fill the blanks with the appropriate words or phrases. ⟲文章展開 (各3点)

Japan is facing the problem of ①(   ). To solve the problem, Japan should
②(   ) foreign workers. Currently, foreign workers can only work for a specific
③(   ) of time. Thus, they are treated as ④(   ) workers, and they miss
some ⑤(   ) to learn more advanced skills. This has led to their poor working
conditions. Foreign people will not choose to work in Japan ⑥(   ) these working
conditions improve.

1 Imagine that you are in a bullet train, the *Shinkansen*. The automatic door of the train car opens, and then you enter and look for a seat. The car has *rows of seats, some for two passengers and some for three passengers. Then, which seat will you choose? If you are going to sit in a seat alone, every available seat becomes your option. You can choose one as you like. Or, (1)you may think that anywhere is fine as long as you can sit down. Now, what will you do if you are in a group of two or more? Surely you don't want to sit far from each other. Actually, the seating *arrangements for two passengers and three passengers can solve (2)this problem.

2 We can explain why the seating arrangement *makes sense from a mathematical point of view. The key point is the following two numbers, " 2" and " 3"; it cannot be 1 or 4 —— it has to be 2 and 3. The seating arrangements for two passengers and three passengers can handle any number of passenger groups. Figure 1 shows, for example, that if you are in a group of four people, you can take two seats which are for two passengers. If a group of five people want to sit together, they can be divided into one seat for two passengers and the other for three passengers. When a group of six people sit together, they can take two seats that are for three passengers. In this way, the seating arrangement is designed to allow various numbers of passenger groups to sit close together.

Figure 1	The seat		Figure 2
👥	■■ □□□		2
👥👤	□□ ■■■		3
👥👥	■■ □□□		4= 2+2
	■■ □□□		
👥👥👤	■■ ■■■		5= 2+3
👥👥👥	□□ ■■■		6= 3+3 (or 2+2+2)
	□□ ■■■		

3 Let's look more closely at the numbers " 2" and " 3." In mathematics, the number " 2" or " 3" are both referred to as "(3)prime numbers." A prime number is a number, like 2 or 3, that can only be divided by its own number, except for 1. For example, 4 is not a prime number because it is divided by its own number 4 and also by 2. As Figure 2 shows, any number can be expressed by adding 2 and 3. (4)The prime numbers " 2" and " 3" are quite fascinating.

row：列　　arrangement：配列（したもの）　　make sense：道理にかなう

本文音声

1. Translate the following into Japanese: (1)you may think that anywhere is fine as long as you can sit down. 　　　　　　　　　　　　　　　　　　　　　　　　知識・技能 （7点）

_____

_____

2. What is (2)this problem? Explain in Japanese. 　　　　　　　指示表現 （8点）

_____

_____

3. What is the definition of the word (3)prime number? Explain in Japanese. キーワードの理解 （7点）

_____

_____

4. Why does the writer say (4)the prime numbers " 2" and " 3" are quite fascinating? Explain in Japanese. 　　　　　　　　　　　　　　　　　　　　まとめの段落 （9点）

_____

_____

5. According to the passage, if a group of 11 people use a *Shinkansen*, what arrangement is appropriate? Paint the squares black to represent the seats the group members will take. 　　　　　　　　　　　　　　　　　　　　　　　　応用 （9点）

☐☐　☐☐☐
☐☐　☐☐☐
☐☐　☐☐☐

6. Which of the following situations does the content of the passage apply to? 　応用 （10点）
   a. Dividing baseball team members into several groups to take taxis which can hold up to four passengers.
   b. Dividing members of a class into some several groups for group discussions.
   c. Providing handouts to students in a classroom with six students per row.
   d. Small tricks performed by two or three cheerleaders before they go on to the next big trick.

Lesson 5

語数（速読目標時間）	関連教科	関連SDGs	得点
383（3分50秒）		3 GOOD HEALTH AND WELL-BEING	
制限時間	家庭		
20分			/ 50

1　Have you ever heard of "young carers," or children who take care of a relative instead of adults? They care for sick family members and do household tasks such as making meals, cleaning, and doing laundry for them, and so on. In Japan, (1)one out of every twenty junior and senior high school students is a young carer.

5　**2**　In 2021, a (2)study about young carers was conducted by the Ministry of Health, Labor and Welfare *in cooperation with the Ministry of Education, Culture, Sports, Science and Technology. According to the study, many young carers look after their *siblings, and nearly 60% of them do so almost every day. It also showed that, on average, young carers are spending four hours a day on care, but some are spending 10　more than seven hours a day. Furthermore, it was pointed out that few of these people are even aware that they are young carers.

3　(3)What kinds of issues can we see in these situations of young carers? First of all, spending a lot of time taking care of their families prevents the carers from having enough time to study. This leads to their poor grades. Some might have to give up on 15　further education or employment. Second, they miss more school, arrive late or leave early more often. As a result, they find it difficult to lead their school life. Another issue is the *isolation of young carers. They cannot participate in club activities after school because they need to take care of their family members. Also, they *hesitate to talk about their situation and care. Therefore, they cannot build good friendships. 20　They are more likely to become isolated in school and feel stressed.

4　(4)The Japanese strong sense of family values —— that families should take care of their family members on their own —— has made the problem of young carers more serious. It is important for family members to support each other. However, we cannot allow heavy *burdens of care to *cloud the futures of young people. We should 25　create a system to support young carers. For example, schools can play an important role in finding out which students are young carers. To provide them with proper supports, schools should strengthen their ties to local government welfare sections. More school social workers are also needed.

---

in cooperation with ... : …と協力[共同]して　　sibling : きょうだい　　isolation : 孤立
hesitate to ～ : ～するのをためらう　　burden : 負担　　cloud : …を曇らせる

本文音声

1. (1)One out of every twenty junior and senior high school students is a young carer has a similar meaning to _____. ⌕ 知識・技能 (8点)

   a. about 8.3% of Japanese students need to be taken care of by others

   b. 5% of Japanese junior and senior high school students are taking care of a relative

   c. in a junior and senior high school class, there are 20 young carers on average

   d. 20% of Japanese junior and senior high school students are young carers

2. Which graph is best supported by the (2)study? ⌕ 指示語 (8点)

   a. きょうだいの世話に費やす時間　　b. きょうだいの世話をする頻度　　c. 自分をヤングケアラーと思うか　　d. 世話をしている家族

3. (3)What kinds of issues can we see in these situations of young carers? Explain each issue briefly in Japanese. ⌕ 段落構成 (各5点)

   · _____

   · _____

   · _____

4. Translate the following into Japanese: (4)The Japanese strong sense of family values —— that families should take care of their family members on their own —— has made the problem of young carers more serious. ⌕ 知識・技能 (9点)

   _____

   _____

5. Which of the following is closest to the writer's opinion? ⌕ 筆者の意見 (10点)

   a. People should support young carers.

   b. The number of young carers should be decreased.

   c. Young carers should be independent from others.

   d. Young carers should focus more on taking care of others than on their schoolwork.

Lesson **6**

語数（速読目標時間）	関連教科	関連SDGs	得　点
375（3分45秒）	—	8 DECENT WORK AND ECONOMIC GROWTH	
制限時間			
20分			/ 50

1　What do you need to be a successful employee or leader?　We tend to think of IQ and technical knowledge as the keys to climbing the *corporate ladder.　However, in today's workplaces, employers assume you have those skills.　What *separates good team members from others is (1)emotional intelligence.　It is a skill set that affects how
5　we treat ourselves and deal with others.

2　The level of one's emotional intelligence is often referred to as one's EQ.　The concept was famously written about by psychologist Daniel Goleman in his 1995 book *Emotional Intelligence*.　Goleman describes several *components of EQ, such as self-awareness, motivation, and *empathy.　People with a high EQ can review their
10　behavior and get along with others.　They're sensitive to the needs of coworkers and customers.　They work well in teams, communicate skillfully, and put maximum effort into their jobs.

3　Having a high or low EQ has an impact on the real world.　Studies of thousands of workers have provided hard data on the subject.　Consider, for example, two qualified
15　people are competing for a job or a promotion.　Research shows that the position will likely go to the person with a higher EQ.　Also, (2)the higher up one goes in a company, the more important the skill set becomes.　Goleman states that, *all in all, EQ is twice as important as IQ.

4　(3)A person's EQ is not set for life.　Bad habits can be changed through (4)hard work.
20　Attending classes or workshops is one method.　For instance, the Weatherhead School of Management offers several emotional-intelligence courses.　People can take classes on working in teams, improving sales techniques, and so on.　There's also a fast-growing industry of "career coaches."　They help *executives and other professionals improve leadership styles and make career decisions.

25　**5**　In fields like sales and customer service, employees clearly benefit from having a well-developed EQ.　But (5)these fields aren't the only ones.　In many local and global businesses, employees need strong *interpersonal and cross-cultural skills.　Large companies like IBM have even built standards like developing personal responsibility into their core set of values.　At the same time, IBM's profits are very healthy.　Clearly,
30　emotional intelligence plays a role in making employees happier and more productive. It also improves the companies' *bottom lines.

---

corporate ladder：出世（の）階段　　separate ... from 〜：〜と…を区別する　　component：構成要素　　empathy：共感
all in all：全般的にみて，概して　　executive：幹部，重役　　interpersonal：人間関係の　　bottom line：最終利益

本文音声

1. What is (1)emotional intelligence? Explain in Japanese.　　　　　　 ✎ 指示語 （7点）

_____

2. Translate the following into Japanese: (2)the higher up one goes in a company, the more important the skill set becomes. 　　　　　　　 ✎ 知識・技能 （7点）

_____

_____

3. Which has the similar meaning to (3)a person's EQ is not set for life?　 ✎ 主題 （7点）
   a. Your EQ can be improved with training.
   b. Your EQ does not matter to your life.
   c. Your EQ is fixed from birth.
   d. Your EQ is determined after you die.

4. What is the (4)hard work for changing your bad habits? Give two methods in Japanese.　　　　　　　　　　　　　　　　　 ✎ 段落構成 （各7点）
   • _____
   • _____

5. Which has a similar meaning to (5)these fields aren't the only ones?　 ✎ 指示語 （7点）
   a. Employees aren't the only ones who benefit from having a well-developed EQ.
   b. Employees benefit not only from having a well-developed EQ, but also from other factors.
   c. Sales and customer service are the fields whose employees benefit not only from having a well-developed EQ, but also from other factors.
   d. Sales and customer service aren't the only fields where employees benefit from having a well-developed EQ.

6. Suppose you were working for a company. What should you do in order to improve your EQ? You may choose more than one option.　　　　　 ✎ 全体把握 （完答8点）
   a. Attend a driving school for large vehicles.
   b. Get a programming certification.
   c. Learn how to improve your designing skills.
   d. Make it a habit to keep a business diary and review it sometimes.
   e. Try to consider the feelings of others when you listen to them.

1 For hundreds of years, ocean travelers have looked to the sky to help navigate their way across oceans. In the 21st century, people still look to the sky for direction, but now they use satellites to identify where they are. In fact, it is quite common to see people using what is called the Global Positioning System (GPS), which is a satellite navigation system, to answer (1)the age-old questions: Where am I? (2)How do I get to where I want to go?

2 The art of navigation has developed into (3)a *sophisticated science from its *primitive beginnings. *Prior to the 15th century, sailors *were reluctant to sail out of sight of land, partly because they feared getting lost and did not know what might be found beyond the horizon. In the early part of the 15th century, Portuguese sailors began to sail farther out into the Atlantic using their knowledge of winds and currents as guides. To sail even farther away from land required an accurate way to measure direction and speed. (4)To measure speed, sailors threw a log into the sea. Attached to the log was a rope which had *knots evenly spaced apart. Sailors would then count the number of knots pulled out from the ship *in a given period of time. From this observation, an approximate speed of the ship could be calculated. (5)The method was not very accurate, yet it was the best that they could do at the time. In fact, Christopher Columbus almost certainly relied on this method to navigate across the Atlantic Ocean.

3 By the *latter half of the 20th century, navigation techniques had improved *considerably. The US military had devised a GPS navigation system that could provide their *missiles with the *coordinates for any point on the surface of the Earth. However, GPS technology was not made available to ordinary citizens until the mid-1990s.

4 Thanks to the introduction of GPS, the age-old problems of knowing where you are and how to get to where you want to go have *essentially been solved. Today, GPS navigation equipment is standard on almost all vehicles.

---

sophisticated：洗練された　　primitive：原始的な　　prior to ...：…より前に　　be reluctant to ～：～したがらない
knot：結び目　　in a given period of time：一定時間に　　latter：後半の　　considerably：かなり，大幅に
missile：ミサイル　　coordinate：座標　　essentially：本質的に

本文音声

1. What is the meaning of (1)the age-old questions? 言いかえ表現 (7点)
   a. The questions that haven't been solved for many years.
   b. The questions that many elderly people ask.
   c. The questions that many people have had since ancient times.
   d. The questions of how old someone or something is.

2. Translate the following into Japanese: (2)How do I get to where I want to go? 知識・技能 (7点)

_____

_____

3. What are the examples of (3)a sophisticated science and primitive beginnings? Answer in English words or phrases. 主題 (各7点)
   a sophisticated science : _____
   primitive beginnings : _____

4. Illustrate the device that sailors used (4)to measure speed in the early part of the 15th century. 内容理解 (7点)

5. Imagine the reason why (5)the method was not very accurate. Explain it in Japanese. 推測 (8点)

_____

_____

6. According to the passage, which of the following is true about GPS? キーワードの理解 (7点)
   a. After it was invented, people stopped looking to the sky for direction.
   b. It became available to ordinary people soon after its debut.
   c. It was originally developed for military purposes.
   d. Its name stands for "Global Positioning Satellite."

1 Japan has become internationalized. The number of foreign people living in Japan has been increasing every year. That number reached approximately 2.93 million in 2019, which is about three times as many as there were 30 years ago. In order to live safely in Japan, foreign residents need to understand the laws and other information provided by the central and local governments.

2 (1)To realize a society where Japanese and non-Japanese can live together, it is important to deliver such information in "easy Japanese" rather than in *multiple languages. "Easy Japanese" refers to a Japanese language that is simpler than ordinary one and easier to understand. (2)An interesting survey was conducted among foreign residents with various *mother tongues in Shizuoka Prefecture. More than 60% answered that they could speak and read simple Japanese. On the other hand, only about 20% chose English as a language necessary for their daily lives. In short, translating information into English, which is regarded as a global language, does not necessarily help foreign people understand it. There is a high need for easy Japanese.

3 The origin of easy Japanese dates back to the Great Hanshin-Awaji Earthquake in 1995. Not only Japanese people but also many foreign people who were in Japan got injured in the earthquake. Some of them couldn't understand Japanese nor English well enough to receive life-saving information. Therefore, easy Japanese was designed to deliver information on natural disasters quickly, accurately, and *briefly so that foreign people could take appropriate actions when a disaster happens.

4 In easy Japanese, for example, "check (*kakunin*)" can be *paraphrased as "look closely (*yoku miru*)." "I am on *childcare leave now," can be translated as "I am off work to raise my child." The following are (3)some rules for easy Japanese. Shorten the length of a sentence and make its structure simple. Use simple words instead of difficult ones. Avoid unclear expressions and *double negatives.

5 Now, many local governments prepare disaster handbooks or hazard maps in easy Japanese for foreign people. All the texts are written in easy Japanese, and the *kanji* are marked with *furigana*. They provide useful information, such as how to *evacuate when a typhoon or earthquake attacks, where the evacuation site is, and what to prepare for a disaster.

6 Recently, easy Japanese has become one of the most effective tools to communicate not only with non-Japanese, but also with children, the elderly, and physically challenged people. Furthermore, for those who send messages, trying to deliver information through easy Japanese can help improve their own communication skills.

本文音声

multiple：多数の　　mother tongue：母語　　briefly：簡潔に　　paraphrase：…を（わかりやすく）言いかえる
childcare leave：育児休暇［休業］　　double negative：二重否定　　evacuate：避難する

1. Which graph shows the correct numbers of foreign people living in Japan?　🏷内容理解（6点）

 a.　　　　 b.　　　　 c.　　　　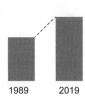 d.

2. Translate the following into Japanese: (1)To realize a society where Japanese and non-Japanese can live together, it is important to deliver such information in "easy Japanese" rather than in multiple languages. Be sure to make "such information" clear.　🏷知識・技能（8点）

_____

_____

3. What are the two questions likely to be included in (2)an interesting survey?　Answer in Japanese.　🏷推測（各7点）

・_____

・_____

4. Which of the following is true about "easy Japanese"?　🏷キーワードの理解（7点）
   a. It was invented just before the Great Hanshin-Awaji Earthquake.
   b. It was originally designed to deliver information on natural disasters.
   c. It was originally invented for small children to understand necessary information.
   d. It was used in schools to improve students' communication skills.

5. According to (3)some rules, which sentence is the best in the situation?　🏷応用（7点）

   Situation: A strong typhoon is approaching. People are ordered to evacuate.
   a. 風がとても強くなるので，海など，安全でないところにいかないでください。
   b. 風がとても強くなります。学校の体育館など，安全なところににげてください。
   c. 猛烈な台風が接近しています。公共施設等の安全な場所に避難してください。
   d. 猛烈な台風が接近しているので，学校の体育館など，安全なところににげてください。

6. Explain "easy Japanese" in about 60 words in Japanese.　🏷要約（8点）

																	60		

1 There is a vast amount of water in the world, but one of the biggest tasks facing engineers today is how to make that water usable. Only 4% of the world's water is fresh and drinkable; the rest is salt water in the ocean. Unfortunately, salt water cannot be used for drinking, cleaning, or even farming.

5 **2** Scientists and engineers are helping people use more and more of the ocean's water. For example, many countries are already using (1)desalination plants to make salt water usable. Desalination is the process where salt is removed from seawater by using filters. One of the ways this is done is by reverse *osmosis. A *membrane is used to separate the salt from the water. Unfortunately, a lot of energy is needed to 10 complete this process. Also, desalination plants are very expensive to build. Therefore, this process is not practical for (2)the people who might need it the most.

3 Currently, engineers are exploring new processes. One consists of (3)a filtering method using *nano-osmosis. This process uses extremely small tubes of carbon called nanotubes. The size of these tubes is on the scale of nanometers, and they are 15 excellent filters. When water is forced through these nanotubes, salt and waste are taken out. These carbon nanotubes could help to solve the problem of water shortages in some areas.

4 Although desalination may help provide fresh drinking water for some people, it may still not be enough to solve the entire problem. Engineers and scientists are also 20 looking at ways to clean waste from water so that it can be recycled. If waste and *pollutants can be removed from water, then that water could be used for farming and other commercial purposes.

5 Another method for providing clean water is water distillation. During distillation, water is boiled to the point of becoming steam. (4)The waste in that water will remain 25 behind so that when the steam becomes liquid again, it is clean and usable. Small, efficient, and economical distillation machines could possibly provide water to an average neighborhood at a small cost.

6 Another engineering issue is the maintenance of water systems already *in place. Many urban areas use very old water systems. Old pipes need to be replaced, and 30 more efficient water systems need to be installed so that clean, fresh water will always be available.

7 Clean, usable water is essential for all human beings. Scientists and engineers are currently working to solve the world's water problems, but until those problems are resolved, we can all help each other by conserving the water we use, one drop at a time.

本文音声

osmosis：浸透　　membrane：膜　　nano：ナノ（［単位］10億分の１）　　pollutant：汚染物質　　in place：実施されて

1. What is the definition of the word (1)desalination? Write a single Japanese word.

🔖 知識・技能 （9点）

(　　　　　　　　　　　)

2. Who are most likely to be (2)the people who might need it the most?　　🔖 推測 （8点）
   a. Scientists and engineers are.
   b. The people who are trying to earn money by building desalination plants are.
   c. The people who have access to clean water are.
   d. The people who live in poor countries with little water are.

3. Explain (3)a filtering method using nano-osmosis in Japanese.　　🔖 主題 （8点）

_____

_____

4. Which of the following is the closest meaning to (4)the waste in that water will remain behind so that when the steam becomes liquid again, it is clean and usable?　　🔖 内容理解 （8点）
   a. Steam will be left behind after the water is boiled. The steam then drops its waste and becomes clean and usable water after becoming a liquid.
   b. Steam will be left behind while the water becomes waste. The waste then becomes clean and usable water after becoming a liquid.
   c. Water will remain behind while the waste becomes steam. The waste then drops liquid so the water is clean and usable.
   d. Waste will remain behind while the water becomes steam. The steam then becomes clean and usable after becoming a liquid.

5. Besides using ocean water and used water, what else can engineers do to solve the world's water problems? Explain in Japanese.　　🔖 文章展開 （10点）

_____

_____

6. In the last paragraph, what the writer wants to say the most is [　　　].　　🔖 主張の意図 （7点）
   a. all we can do is wait for the arrival of new technologies in order to solve the water problems
   b. new technologies will solve the world's water problems and we won't have to worry about them
   c. people who are not scientists or engineers can help solve the world's water problems
   d. scientists and engineers are key to solving the world's water problems

1 Everyone knows that running is a good way to stay in shape. The simplicity of running appeals to many people. You don't need a lot of expensive equipment; you just need a good pair of running shoes. Well, (1)that idea is changing. Some researchers suggest that perhaps you do not need shoes at all.

5 **2** This is not a surprise to the Tarahumara Native Americans, who live in northwestern Mexico. The rough ground in their area makes it easier to travel on foot than by car. Traditionally, the Tarahumara were hunters. They followed the animals that they were hunting for long distances, sometimes for days, until the animals became tired and died. As a result, for the Tarahumara, running very long distances 10 became part of daily life. They are known for their *stamina, running races of 50 miles (80 kilometers) or longer. When Tarahumara athletes ran in the marathon at the 1968 Olympics, they did not understand that the race was over after only 26. 2 miles, so they kept running. "Too short," they complained.

3 But here is the amazing part: Tarahumara runners don't wear running shoes. 15 (2)Tarahumara shoes are very simple. The *sole is a piece of *rubber held to the foot with homemade straps. These rubber shoes protect their feet against sharp objects, but they don't provide any support or cushioning.

4 How is it possible that some of the best runners in the world don't wear running shoes? Scientific studies are beginning to look at something the Tarahumara have 20 known for centuries: (3)human bodies are made for running *barefoot. In a recent study, researchers used a video camera to see how athletes run when they are barefoot. The study made it clear that barefoot runners land on the middle of their foot. When they do this, the *arch of the foot reduces the impact. Then that force is sent back up through the leg.

25 **5** As we look at the side view of a barefoot runner, (4)we can understand why this makes sense. The barefoot *stride has two clear advantages over running in shoes. First, the raised arch is the foot's shock reducer. As the force of impact pushes the foot toward the ground, the arch becomes flat and wider. It reduces the energy of impact. Second, as the foot leaves the ground, that energy travels back up the leg. This helps 30 the leg move upward into the next step. One way to understand this is to imagine the arch as a trampoline. The downward movement is switched to an upward force, increasing the runner's speed.

---

stamina：持久力　　sole：靴底　　rubber：ゴム　　barefoot：裸足で[の]　　arch of a foot：土踏まず　　stride：歩幅，一歩

本文音声

1. (1)That idea is changing means ☐. 🖉 主題 (7点)
  a. if you want to enjoy running, you may need expensive equipment in addition to your shoes
  b. running doesn't appeal to many people anymore
  c. you may not even need a pair of shoes for running
  d. you should buy expensive and good running shoes

2. How far can the Tarahumara Native Americans run? Why did they become able to run such a long distance? Explain in Japanese. 🖉 原因と結果 (各7点)
どのくらいの距離を走ることができるか：＿＿＿＿＿＿＿＿＿＿＿＿＿＿＿＿＿＿＿
なぜ長距離を走ることができるようになったか：＿＿＿＿＿＿＿＿＿＿＿＿＿＿＿
＿＿＿＿＿＿＿＿＿＿＿＿＿＿＿＿＿＿＿＿＿＿＿＿＿＿＿＿＿＿＿＿＿＿＿＿＿＿

3. Illustrate (2)Tarahumara shoes. 🖉 内容理解 (7点)

4. Why can we say (3)human bodies are made for running barefoot? Explain in detail in Japanese. 🖉 主張と根拠 (8点)
＿＿＿＿＿＿＿＿＿＿＿＿＿＿＿＿＿＿＿＿＿＿＿＿＿＿＿＿＿＿＿＿＿＿＿＿＿＿
＿＿＿＿＿＿＿＿＿＿＿＿＿＿＿＿＿＿＿＿＿＿＿＿＿＿＿＿＿＿＿＿＿＿＿＿＿＿

5. Translate the following into Japanese: (4)we can understand why this makes sense. Be sure to make "this" clear. 🖉 知識・技能 (7点)
＿＿＿＿＿＿＿＿＿＿＿＿＿＿＿＿＿＿＿＿＿＿＿＿＿＿＿＿＿＿＿＿＿＿＿＿＿＿
＿＿＿＿＿＿＿＿＿＿＿＿＿＿＿＿＿＿＿＿＿＿＿＿＿＿＿＿＿＿＿＿＿＿＿＿＿＿

6. Which of the following is true about the passage? 🖉 全体把握 (7点)
  a. In some of the latest running shoes, you may feel as if you are running barefoot.
  b. In the 1968 Olympics, some barefoot runners showed remarkable performances.
  c. Jumping on a trampoline may make you a better runner.
  d. Under some circumstances, running barefoot may be better than running in shoes.

Lesson 11

語数(速読目標時間)　465(4分40秒)
制限時間　20分
関連教科　地理歴史・公民
関連SDGs　5 GENDER EQUALITY　16 PEACE, JUSTICE AND STRONG INSTITUTIONS
得　点　／50

1 Have you ever heard the name, Ruth Bader Ginsburg or RBG? (1)She is such a popular American woman that you may see some goods with her picture and famous words on them, for example, T-shirts, coffee mugs, and even little RBG dolls. Who was RBG? A hip-hop singer? A movie star? She was the second female justice on the
5 *United States Supreme Court. During her life, she tried hard to correct unfair laws that treated men and women differently.

2 In 1933, Ruth was born to a Jewish *immigrant family in Brooklyn, New York. Her mother, Cecelia, loved Ruth very much. Even though Cecelia could not receive a proper education, she taught Ruth a lot of things. She often told Ruth that girls are as
10 important as boys. She wanted Ruth to study hard and get a good education.

3 Back then in America, life was much harder for people who were different. Ruth faced a lot of unfair treatment simply because she was (2)left-handed, Jewish, and a woman. Despite receiving such unfair treatment, she never gave up and made great efforts to overcome (3)discrimination. She soon realized that there were many people
15 who were treated as unfairly as she was. At college, Ruth studied to be a lawyer. This job can help people by *standing up for their rights in a court of law. In 1980, she became a *federal judge in Washington D.C., and in 1993 she became a U.S. Supreme Court Justice.

4 Early in her career as Justice Ginsburg, she made a decision on one of the most
20 important cases in American history. In 1989, a female high school student from northern Virginia applied to enter the Virginia Military Institute (VMI). VMI is the oldest military college in the United States, and it was a college that admitted only male students. Therefore, the female student was rejected simply because she was a woman. Seven years later, in 1996, the U.S. Supreme Court heard the student's
25 complaint and ruled that the VMI's admission policy was against the *Constitution of the United States.

5 Justice Ginsburg and six other justices decided that the traditional admission policy of VMI was wrong. Above all, Justice Ginsburg supported women's rights clearly. She explained that any law which denies women something because of their
30 gender is *unconstitutional. She insisted that all women should be treated equally and given equal opportunities to "participate in and contribute to society based on their individual talents and capacities." In September of that year, VMI's male-only admissions policy came to an end.

6 In 2020, Justice Ginsburg passed away from cancer at the age of 87. She was a

本文音声

35 person with a strong belief that laws should be fair and should protect people's rights, no matter who they are, what they believe, and where they come from.

> United States Supreme Court：アメリカ合衆国最高裁判所　　immigrant：移民(の)
> stand up for ...：…を弁護する[守る]　　federal：アメリカ連邦政府の　　Constitution：憲法
> unconstitutional：憲法に反する

1. Translate the following into Japanese: (1)She is such a popular American woman that you may see some goods with her picture and famous words on them.　✎ 知識・技能 (8点)

_____

_____

2. Which of the following was true about Ruth?　✎ 主題 (6点)
   a. She studied law at college to become a lawyer.
   b. She wanted to study and get a proper education.
   c. She was an immigrant from Brooklyn, New York.
   d. She was the first female justice on the United States Supreme Court.

3. In paragraph 3, what is the single word that describes (2)left-handed, Jewish, and a woman?　✎ 抽象と具体 (7点)

   (　　　　　　　　　)

4. In paragraph 3, what phrase is closest in meaning to (3)discrimination?　✎ 言いかえ表現 (7点)

   _____

5. Explain the case of the VMI from the three viewpoints below in Japanese.　✎ 内容理解 (各5点)
   訴訟内容：_____
   _____
   判決結果：_____
   _____
   VMI の対応：_____
   _____

6. What did Justice Ginsburg think about laws? Explain in detail in Japanese.
   ✎ 知識・技能 ✎ まとめの段落 (7点)

_____

_____

_____

Lesson 12

語数（速読目標時間）	関連教科	関連SDGs	得 点
429(4分15秒)	理科	14 LIFE BELOW WATER　15 LIFE ON LAND	
制限時間 20分			/ 50

1 Endangered species are wildlife that is in danger of extinction. (1)Once gone, they are gone forever, and there is no bringing them back. Losing even a single species can have great impacts on a whole ecosystem. This is because the effects will be felt throughout the food chain. (2)The causes include a decrease in the number and size of

5 *habitats due to development, overhunting, and environmental pollution that has greatly reduced the number of *inhabitants. In recent years, the effects of habitat change and loss due to global warming and non-native animals and plants introduced by people have also become serious.

2 The International Union for Conservation of Nature (IUCN) *compiles a list of

10 endangered species into a database called the (3)Red List. The list is updated *from time to time based on the results of surveys of wildlife by a group of researchers in each specialized field. The ranks of the crisis are divided into the following forms:

Extinct [EX]	beyond reasonable doubt that the species is already extinct
Extinct in the Wild [EW]	survives only in human care and/or outside native range
Critically Endangered [CR]	in a particularly and extremely critical state
Endangered [EN]	very high risk of extinction in the wild
Vulnerable [VU]	considered to be at high risk of unnatural (human-caused) extinction without further human treatment
Near Threatened [NT]	close to being at high risk of extinction in the near future
Least Concern [LC]	unlikely to become extinct in the near future
Data Deficient [DD]	lack of information to evaluate
Not Evaluated [NE]	

Among these, "endangered wildlife" generally refers to wildlife ranked in three categories ([CR] Critically Endangered, [EN] Endangered, and [VU] Vulnerable).

15 **3** *As of December 2020, the (4)IUCN Red List of Threatened Species included more than 35,765 species of wildlife in these three categories. That number is 28% of the total number of species (128,918) evaluated by the IUCN. The IUCN Red List specifically identifies *mammals, birds, and *amphibians in danger. For example, among the 5,932 mammal species, 1,317 are endangered. This means that more than

20 20% of the species are threatened with extinction. Among the 11,158 bird species, 1,481, or 13%, are threatened. And among the 7,166 amphibian species, 2,390, or 33%, are threatened.

4 What is worse, the IUCN has not yet studied fishes and *invertebrates sufficiently. Further research on them may reveal that a lot more species are at risk of extinction. It

25 is important to remember that the numbers shown in the Red List are only a partial picture of the critical state of wildlife in the world as a whole.

habitat：生息地　　inhabitant：居住者　　compile ... into ～：…を～にまとめる　　from time to time：ときどき［随時］
as of ...：…の時点で　　mammal：哺乳類　　amphibian：両生類　　invertebrate：無脊椎動物

1. Translate the following into Japanese: (1)Once gone, they are gone forever, and there is no bringing them back. Be sure to make "they" clear.　　✎ 知識・技能 （9点）

_____

_____

2. Among (2)the causes, what has started to have a serious impact on wildlife recently? Explain in Japanese.　　✎ 論理 （9点）

_____

_____

3. Which of the following is true about the (3)Red List?　　✎ キーワードの理解 （7点）
   a. Fishes and invertebrates have not been added to the list yet.
   b. It divides the ranks of the crisis into three categories.
   c. It is made by a few researchers specializing in various fields.
   d. It is sometimes updated according to the results of wildlife surveys.

4. According to the (4)IUCN Red List of Threatened Species, which of the following can be said?　　✎ キーワードの理解 （7点）
   a. About 20% of mammals are threatening animals of other species.
   b. Among 128,918 species, 35,765 have already become extinct.
   c. 1,481 bird species are ranked in "Critically Endangered," "Endangered," or "Vulnerable."
   d. Amphibians are so vulnerable to habitat change that 33% of them are threatened with extinction.

5. According to the writer, what are the two problems about wildlife? Explain in Japanese.　　✎ 文章展開 （各9点）

   · _____

   · _____

語数(速読目標時間)	関連教科	関連SDGs	得 点
471(4分45秒)	—	—	
制限時間			
20分			/ 50

世界で最も成功している人たちは，どのように成功への道を切り開いてきたのでしょうか。以下のオバマ元大統領の演説の中に，そのヒントが隠されているかもしれません。

1 I know that sometimes you may think you can be rich and successful without any hard work. You may think that your ticket to success is through *rapping or basketball or being a reality TV star. (1)Chances are you're not going to be any of those things.

2 The truth is, being successful is hard. You won't love every subject that you study.
5 You won't *click with every teacher that you have. Not every homework will seem completely related to your life. And, you won't necessarily succeed at everything the first time you try.

3 That's okay. Some of the most successful people in the world are the ones who've had the most failures. J. K. Rowling —— who wrote *Harry Potter* —— her first *Harry*
10 *Potter* book was rejected twelve times before it was finally published. Michael Jordan was cut from his high school basketball team. He lost hundreds of games and missed thousands of shots during his career. But he once said, "I have failed over and over and over again in my life. And (2)that's why I succeed."

4 These people succeeded because they understood that you can't let your failures
15 *define you —— you have to let your failures teach you. (3)You have to let them show you what to do differently the next time. So, if you get into trouble, that doesn't mean you're a troublemaker. It means you need to try harder to act right. If you get a bad grade, that doesn't mean you're stupid. It just means you need to spend more time studying.

20 **5** No one is born being good at all things. You become good at things through hard work. You're not a professional athlete the first time you play a new sport. You don't hit every *note the first time you sing a song. You've got to practice. The same principle applies to your schoolwork. You might have to do a math problem a few times before you get the right answer. You might have to read something a few times
25 before you understand it. You definitely have to do a few *drafts of a paper before it's good enough to hand in.

6 Don't be afraid to ask questions. Don't be afraid to ask for help when you need it. I (4)do that every day. Asking for help isn't a sign of weakness. It's a sign of strength because it shows you have the courage to admit that you don't know something. It
30 then allows you to learn something new. So find an adult that you trust —— a parent, a grandparent or teacher, a coach or a counselor —— and ask them to help you *stay on track to meet your goals. And even when you're struggling, even when you're

本文音声

discouraged and you feel like other people have given up on you, don't ever give up on yourself.

rapping：ラップを歌うこと　　click with ...：…とうまくやっていく　　define：…を定義する　　note：音符
draft：下書き　　stay on track：順調に物事を進める

1. Translate the following into Japanese: (1)Chances are you're not going to be any of those things. Be sure to make "those things" clear. 知識・技能（9点）

_____

_____

2. Which has the most similar meaning to (2)that's why I succeed? 原因と結果（8点）
   a. As Obama had failed many times before he became President, he was regarded as one of the best Presidents ever.
   b. J. K. Rowling had her book rejected several times, which made it more attractive.
   c. Michael Jordan became a great player because he lost less games and missed less shots than other players.
   d. Thanks to many mistakes he had made in basketball, Michael Jordan became one of the best basketball players.

3. Translate the following into Japanese: (3)You have to let them show you what to do differently the next time. Be sure to make "them" clear. 知識・技能（9点）

_____

_____

4. What does (4)do that mean? Fill in each blank in English. 指示語（8点）
   I (　　　　　　　　　) (　　　　　　　　　) (　　　　　　　　　) every day.

5. Which of the following is not the main message of this speech? 主題（8点）
   a. You may think you can be rich and successful without any hard work.
   b. Being successful is hard.
   c. You become good at things through hard work.
   d. Don't be afraid to ask for help when you need it.

6. Which of the following was the most likely audience for this speech? 言語の使用場面（8点）
   a. All the students who had just started their new schoolyear.
   b. Americans who had voted for Obama's political party.
   c. Anti-war activists gathered in a square.
   d. *Hibakusha* and their children in Hiroshima and Nagasaki.

Lesson 14

語数(速読目標時間)	関連教科	関連SDGs	得 点
461(4分40秒)	理科	13 CLIMATE ACTION / 14 LIFE BELOW WATER	/ 50
制限時間 20分			

1 Scary music plays. Someone is swimming in the ocean when, suddenly, a *triangular shape rises behind them. The music gets louder and more frightening, but the person on the screen doesn't notice. The shape gets closer and closer, then sinks beneath the waves. Moments later, the person starts to struggle and scream, then
5 disappears into the silent sea.

2 (1)This is the idea that most people have about sharks, based on their appearances in popular films, documentaries and video games. They are often seen as terrifying killers with huge teeth, frighteningly deadly eyes and powerful bodies. However, this is not the whole truth and is actually (2)quite unfair. In reality, sharks are an important
10 part of a healthy ocean, and therefore a healthy planet.

3 Sharks are predators, which means they hunt other fish for food. When they do so, they control the size and increase the diversity of fish populations. This helps to maintain balance. With no sharks, other species can become *dominant and change the marine environment. In addition, as a 2020 study by the ARC Centre of Excellence
15 for Coral Reef Studies found, many sharks, *along with other large fish such as tuna and *swordfish, can act to reduce the amount of carbon dioxide in the atmosphere. When such fish die, they sink to the bottom of the ocean, trapping and storing the carbon inside their bodies.

4 Some sharks are "apex predators," or hunters who are at the top of their natural
20 food chain. There is one very dangerous animal that can threaten their survival, however. This is, of course, the human being. We kill an estimated one hundred million sharks every year. More than half of these are fished for their *fins, which are traditionally used in soup in countries such as China and Vietnam. The rest are caught for their meat, for sport or are accidentally trapped in large fishing nets.

25 **5** (3)When this happens, it has a huge effect not just on them, but on all life in the ocean. Things get out of balance. Because sharks are slow to grow to full size and don't usually have a lot of babies, their populations often cannot recover from overfishing, and many species are close to extinction. In addition, that trapped carbon dioxide mentioned before gets released when the shark's body is cut open and causes
30 further environmental damage.

6 In recent years, more and more attention has been paid to the importance that these magnificent creatures have for the whole planet, as well as the problems that arise when their *existence is under threat. Now, *long-overdue (4)laws are being *put in place to reduce the problems we have caused through our *greed. Still, (5)a lot more

本文音声

35 needs to be managed if we want to reverse the damage already done.

triangular：三角形の　　dominant：優勢な　　along with ...：…と一緒に　　swordfish：メカジキ　　fin：ヒレ
existence：存在，存続　　long-overdue：もっと早くすべきだった　　put ... in place：…を施行する　　greed：欲望

1. What does (1)this mean? Explain in 70-90 words in Japanese.

			70																
	90																		

2. Why does the writer say (2)quite unfair? Explain in Japanese. 🗨論理 (9点)

_____

_____

3. How can sharks reduce the amount of carbon dioxide in the atmosphere? Explain in Japanese. 🗨知識・技能 (9点)

_____

4. Translate the following into Japanese: (3)When this happens, it has a huge effect not just on them, but on all life in the ocean. Be sure to make "this" and "them" clear. 🗨指示語 (9点)

_____

_____

5. Which of the following is most likely to be the example of (4)laws? 🗨言いかえ表現 (7点)
   a. A law that allows local workers to establish shark farms.
   b. A law that bans fishers and fishing companies from catching any sharks.
   c. A law that establishes an area where no foreign ships are allowed to enter without permission.
   d. A law that restricts the amount of yearly catch of fish and shellfish.

6. As to the underlined part (5), what is a lot more and the damage already done? 🗨内容理解 (7点)

	a lot more	the damage already done
a.	Stricter and further laws	Climate change
b.	Stricter and further laws	Overfishing of sharks
c.	The number of sharks	Climate change
d.	The number of sharks	Overfishing of sharks

Lesson
15

語数（速読目標時間）	関連教科	関連SDGs	得　点
462（4分40秒）	地理歴史・公民	10 REDUCED INEQUALITIES　16 PEACE, JUSTICE AND STRONG INSTITUTIONS	
制限時間			
20分			/ 50

1 Rosa Parks took a historic stand against *racial segregation when she refused to give up her bus seat to a white man in Montgomery, Alabama, on December 1, 1955.

2 The "Mother of the Civil Rights Movement" was not the first person to fight against segregation.　It wasn't even the first time that Parks met James F. Blake.　(1)He was the bus driver who had Parks arrested when she refused to give up her seat to a white passenger.　But civil rights leaders were able to use Parks' stand as a reason for (2)the Montgomery bus boycott and the larger civil rights movement.

3 Her first conflict with driver Blake was nearly a decade before the incident.　When Blake was driving a bus, Parks got on and paid her fare.　Blake told Parks to exit and enter again through the back doors because it was common for Black passengers at the time.　When she got off the bus via the front door to walk to the back, Blake drove the bus away.　He left Parks behind at the bus stop.

4 The two would come face-to-face with each other again on December 1, 1955.　The 42-year-old Parks was ordered by Blake to move out of her seat on the crowded bus so that a white man could sit there.　Three other Black passengers moved, but (3)Parks stayed in her seat.　She was arrested for this behavior.

5 Thinking back on the event later, she wrote, "I had been *pushed around all my life, and I felt at this moment I couldn't stand it any longer."　Her arrest led to the peaceful Montgomery bus boycott.　It lasted 381 days and helped make then-26-year-old Martin Luther King, Jr. nationally known as the leader of civil rights movement.

6 Parks was guilty in the case.　While her appeal *made its way through the court system, however, on June 4, 1956, the District Court ruled that racial segregation of public buses was unconstitutional.　The Supreme Court supported the decision on November 13, 1956.

7 The Montgomery bus boycott was the first of many racial justice *protests that Parks participated in.　She took part in the *March on Washington for Jobs and Freedom in 1963 and the famous *Selma-to-Montgomery March in 1965.

8 Parks eventually went to work for the district office of John Conyers from 1965-1988.　After retiring, she received the Presidential Medal of Freedom from President Bill Clinton in 1996.　She also received the *Congressional Gold Medal in 1999.

9 "Rosa Parks said, 'I didn't get on that bus to get arrested.　I got on that bus to go home.'　In so many ways, Rosa Parks brought America home, to our Founder's dream," Clinton said in 1999 when he presented Parks with the medal.

10 Parks died in 2005 at the age of 92.

本文音声

racial segregation：人種分離［差別］　　push ... around：…をこき使う［振り回す］
make one's way through ...：…を通り抜ける［進む］　　protest：抗議（運動）
March on Washington for Jobs and Freedom：ワシントン大行進（ワシントンでおこなわれた人種差別撤廃を求める行進）
Selma-to-Montgomery March：セルマ大行進（アフリカ系アメリカ人の選挙権獲得を求める行進）
congressional：アメリカ議会の

1. Translate the following into Japanese: (1)He was the bus driver who had Parks arrested
   when she refused to give up her seat to a white passenger.　　　▷ 知識・技能 （7点）

   _____

   _____

2. Which of the following is true about (2)the Montgomery bus boycott?　　▷ 主題 （6点）
   a. Many whites and blacks were injured and killed during the boycott.
   b. Parks was in prison and couldn't participate in the boycott.
   c. The boycott ended within a year.
   d. The boycott made Martin Luther King, Jr. famous as the leader of civil rights movement.

3. Describe the two conflicts between Parks and Blake in detail in Japanese.　　▷ 段落構成 （各7点）
   The first conflict :_____

   _____

   The second conflict : _____

   _____

4. What did she think when (3)Parks stayed in her seat? Explain in Japanese.　　▷ 文章展開 （7点）

   _____

   _____

5. After the incident on the bus, what was Parks' life like? Fill the blanks with appropriate
   words to complete the timeline.　　▷ 論理 （各2点）

1956	The District and Supreme Courts banned racial ①(　　　　) in public buses.
1960s	Parks took part in several ②(　　　　) against racial discrimination.
1970s	Parks worked for the district ③(　　　　) of a politician.
1990s	Parks was given ④(　　　　) from the U.S. nation.
⑤(　　　　)	Parks passed away at the age of 92.

6. Which of the following is the best title for this passage?　　▷ 要約 （6点）
   a. American Society —— Breaking Down Racial Barriers
   b. Bill Clinton —— The Challenge for Integrating Black and White
   c. Rosa Parks and the Battle against Segregation
   d. Rosa Parks and the Spiteful Bus Driver

語数(速読目標時間)	関連教科	関連SDGs	得 点
495(5分)	家庭	3 GOOD HEALTH AND WELL-BEING	
制限時間			
20分			/ 50

1 Most people know that eating good food is one of the most important elements for health. The expression (1)"you are what you eat" sums up this idea. If you eat unhealthy food, you will probably become unhealthy. Today, especially in wealthy countries, eating too much food and eating unhealthy kinds of foods have resulted in a

5 wide range of major health problems like *obesity, *diabetes, and allergies. Being aware of such problems is necessary, but thinking only of these dangers can be *somewhat depressing. It seems we need a more positive way to think about good eating.

2 (2)The Slow Food movement encourages people to think about not only what we

10 eat, but how we eat. It grew out of a realization that (3)not only are modern people eating the wrong kinds of food —— junk foods, processed foods, and fast foods —— but also we are rushing our eating and not enjoying our lives. Fast eating takes away the joy of eating. It leads us to ignore the culture of food, our relationship to the farmers who grow our food, and the health of our environment which is necessary for growing

15 good food. The Slow Food movement encourages us to share the experience of eating with other people in a *leisurely way.

3 The Slow Food movement, which started in the 1980s in Italy, (4)uses the snail as its symbol. As the Italian Francesco Angelita wrote in 1607, the snail is an animal "of slow motion, to educate us that being fast makes people rude and foolish." The founders of

20 the Slow Food movement felt that the snail's habit of slowness provided an important message for people today. They realized that the snail has something to teach modern people, who are often too *impatient to feel and taste.

4 Slow Food groups have now spread to countries on five *continents around the world, including Japan. The movement *emphasizes respect for the different local

25 food cultures of each country and local area. It also supports the existence of small-scale farmers who use traditional, *organic methods. It encourages people to buy as much of their food from local farmers as possible, rather than buying imported foods and foods grown on huge "factory farms." The movement reminds us that our attitudes toward food, diet, and health must be connected to caring for a healthy

30 environment where our food is grown. Factory farms may offer us slightly lower prices at the store. But this *initial "benefit" often comes at the greater cost of our personal health, the health of ecosystems, and the health of the local culture. Factory farms and the unhealthy ecosystems they lead to are a part of our overly-fast lives.

5 In a world that seems to continually race faster and faster, the ideas of the Slow

本文音声

35 Food movement may help us to take a healthier attitude toward food, people, culture, time, and the world around us. And they may help us to face the big question: [X   ]?

> obesity：肥満　　diabetes：糖尿病　　somewhat：やや，いくぶん　　leisurely：ゆっくりした
> impatient：我慢できない，せっかちな　　continent：大陸　　emphasize：…を強調する　　organic：有機栽培の
> initial：最初の

1. What does the writer mean by saying (1)"you are what you eat"? Explain in Japanese.

◇ 論理 （8点）

_____

2. When the sentence (2)the Slow Food movement encourages people to think about not only what we eat, but how we eat is read aloud, which word is likely to be emphasized the most?

◇ 文章展開 （8点）

(   )

3. Translate the following into Japanese: (3)not only are modern people eating the wrong kinds of food —— junk foods, processed foods, and fast foods —— but also we are rushing our eating and not enjoying our lives.

◇ 知識・技能 （10点）

_____

_____

4. Why does the Slow Food movement (4)use the snail as its symbol? Explain in Japanese.

◇ 主題 （9点）

_____

_____

5. Which is <u>not</u> true about small-scale farmers and huge "factory farms"?　　◇ 内容理解 （7点）
   a. "Factory farms" go against the idea of the Slow Food movement.
   b. Foods from huge "factory farms" may be "unhealthy kinds of foods."
   c. Small-scale farmers are supported by Slow Food groups.
   d. Small-scale farmers use organic methods, which lowers food prices.

6. The phrase which best suits for [X] is [   ].　　◇ 論理 （8点）
   a. How should we eat
   b. What is life for
   c. What is "Slow Food"
   d. What should we eat

1 The world's most (1)walkable cities include London, Paris, Bogotá and Hong Kong, according to a report by the Institute for Transportation and Development Policy (ITDP). The institute researched almost 1,000 cities around the world about citizens' accessibility to car-free spaces, schools and healthcare, and the shortness of journeys.

5 **2** Researchers at the ITDP said making cities walkable is important to improve health, cut climate-warming transport emissions and build stronger local communities and economies. However, they said most of the cities don't give *pedestrians *priority and are dominated by cars. The report found US cities ranked particularly low for walkability due to *urban sprawl.

10 **3** Among cities with populations of more than 5 million, only Bogotá in Colombia was in the top five for all (2)three measures. The first measure focused on the percentage of people living within 100 meters of a car-free place, such as parks, pedestrian streets and squares. These places improve health, strengthen community connections and increase pedestrian safety, the researchers said. Hong Kong ranked first with 85% within 100 15 meters. Moscow, Paris and London were the other top five cities.

4 The second measure looked at the percentage of people living within a kilometer of both healthcare and education. In Paris, 85% of people live within this distance. The city was followed by Lima in Peru, London, Santiago in Chile and Bogotá.

5 The average size of city blocks was the third measure. Smaller blocks make it 20 easier for people to walk directly to their destinations without going around large buildings. Here, Khartoum in Sudan scored highest. It was followed by Bogotá, Lima, Karachi in Pakistan and Tokyo in Japan.

6 The report shows that (3)places where walking is easier and safer have lower air pollution, less obesity, more children's playtime, fewer road deaths and better 25 performing local businesses, as well as reduced inequality. It notes that nearly 230,000 pedestrians around the world are expected to be killed in road crashes this year.

7 "In order to provide safe and comfortable walking conditions, it is essential to shift the balance of space in our cities away from cars," said Heather Thompson, the head of the ITDP. The ITDP said (4)the need was particularly urgent as the *coronavirus pandemic 30 was driving people away from walking and public transport and into private cars.

8 "Our city streets across the planet are already full of cars," said Taylor Reich, an ITDP researcher. "If you really want to see the worst for walkability, it is the really sprawling cities of the US. They might have great sidewalks, but everything is so far apart that it's impossible to walk to the supermarket or the school."

35 **9** Indianapolis was the lowest ranked US city. Just 4% of people are close to education and healthcare and 9% are next to a car-free area. Reich said *policymakers everywhere need to plan mixes of housing, shops and businesses and provide streets

with benches, wide *pavements and shade.

pedestrian：歩行者　　priority：優先すること
urban sprawl：（都市の）スプロール現象（都心部から郊外へ無秩序・無計画に開発が広がる現象）
coronavirus pandemic：コロナウイルス感染症の大流行　　policymaker：政策立案者　　pavement：舗装道路

1. The word (1)walkable means ☐.　　　　　　　　　　　　　　　　主題 （5点）
   a. being able to move using vehicles and other transportation
   b. being able to move with one's legs
   c. being allowed to let animals such as pets go freely
   d. being easy for people to go around without using vehicles

2. What are the (2)three measures? Explain each of them in Japanese.　　文章展開 （各5点）
   The first measure : _____
   The second measure : _____
   The third measure : _____

3. Based on the (2)three measures, which area (a.～d.) is the most walkable?　　内容理解 （5点）

4. Explain six advantages of (3)places where walking is easier and safer in brief Japanese.
　　　　　　　　　　　　　　　　　　　　　　　　　　　　　　　内容理解 （各2点）

   ・_____　　・_____　　・_____
   ・_____　　・_____　　・_____

5. Explain the reason why (4)the need was particularly urgent in Japanese.　　知識・技能 （7点）
   _____
   _____

6. One opinion from the passage is that ☐.　　　　　　　　　　　事実と意見 （6点）
   a. Bogotá in Colombia was in the top five for all three measures
   b. Indianapolis was the lowest ranked US city
   c. policymakers need to provide streets with benches, wide pavements and shade
   d. the ITDP researched almost 1,000 cities around the world

❶ (1)All children have the right to learn, whatever their circumstances may be. Adequate support for learning is essential if educators want children to develop to their full potential.　Quality education is central to the development of *inclusive societies.　However, in Cambodia, many girls and boys are struggling to learn and
5　realize their potential, particularly those from poor rural families.

❷　Cambodia is known as a success story in education reform.　Great progress has been made since the 1970s, with remarkable expansion in children's access to education.　Today, more Cambodian children are entering school than ever before. Since 2007, the number of children in *early childhood education has more than
10　doubled.　The number of children entering primary education increased from 82% in 1997 to over 97% in the school year 2017/ 18.

❸　Despite this progress, in Cambodia, many children are not reaching age-appropriate learning standards.　At the primary level, nearly 25% of children in Grade 3 cannot write a single word in a *dictation test.　A child who started Grade 1 in the
15　school year 2016/ 17 has a 51% chance of reaching Grade 9.

❹　Main factors behind these include children who are not prepared for school, financial difficulties within families, and the poor quality of teaching.　These factors eventually lead to lacking motivation to attend school.

❺　Education is important for the development of Cambodia.　As one third of its
20　citizens are under 15 years of age, Cambodia has one of the youngest populations in Southeast Asia.　The country's development strategy focuses on its young, dynamic and mobile population as a major *contributor to sustainable development and economic growth.　In (2)the Country Program 2019-2023, the country focuses its efforts on early childhood and basic education together with UNICEF and other partners.
25　They continue to work to ensure that children go to and stay in school, and importantly, learn well while they are there.

❻　The program provides technical and financial support to the government to equip schools with water, sanitation and hand-washing facilities.　This is because children in schools, especially *adolescent girls, without adequate water and sanitation facilities
30　are more likely to attend irregularly or to drop out.

❼　The program also helps the Cambodian government change the national curriculum, including the *syllabus, learning standards, teacher training and textbooks. One of the priorities is to include health, nutrition and life skills in the curriculum so that students can learn how to become healthy, capable and responsible adults.

35 **8** Effective leadership and management of school leaders and teachers are needed as well. Financial aid has been provided for teacher training. This fund helps school leaders and teachers plan and *distribute their resources more effectively. Qualified teachers who can speak multiple languages for *ethnic minority children, and skilled teachers to teach children with *disabilities are particularly needed because they can
40 ensure that schools are places where children's talents are *nurtured and all children can learn.

9 Real progress comes from involving families and communities. It is important to promote education among families and improve how parents value education. It will stimulate a demand for education services so that girls and boys will be encouraged by
45 parents and communities to attend and complete early childhood and basic education.

---

inclusive：包括的な　　early childhood education：幼児教育　　dictation：書き取り，ディクテーション
contributor：功労者　　adolescent：思春期の　　syllabus：教育計画，シラバス
distribute：…を配布[分配]する　　ethnic：民族(集団)の　　disability：身体障害　　nurture：…を育てる[養成する]

1. Translate the following into Japanese: (1)All children have the right to learn, whatever their circumstances may be. ✑ 知識・技能 （6点）

_____

_____

2. According to paragraphs 2 and 3, what are the progress and the failure in educating Cambodian children? Explain each of them in detail in Japanese. ✑ 段落構成 （各8点）

Progress :_____

_____

_____

Failure :_____

_____

_____

3. Which of the reasons below does not make Cambodian children struggle to learn?

✑ 論理 （6点）

  a. Bad result of a dictation test.   b. Financial problems of families.
  c. No adequate preparation for school.   d. Poor quality teaching.

4. What does (2)the Country Program do in order to ensure that children learn well while they are in school? Give three examples in Japanese. ✑ 文章展開 （各4点）

  • _____

   _____

  • _____

   _____

  • _____

   _____

5. For real progress in Cambodian education, what does the writer think is most important? Explain with the reason in Japanese in about 120 words. ✑ まとめの段落 （10点）

120

SDGs 関連語句特集

SDGs は，2015年9月の国連サミットで採択された「持続可能な開発のための2030アジェンダ」にて記載された2030年までに持続可能でよりよい世界を目指す国際目標です。17のゴールと169のターゲットから構成されています。ここでは，169のターゲットに使われる語句をピックアップしました。1.3や1.b などは，その単語が出現するターゲットを表します（アルファベットはターゲットを達成するための手段とされています）。

貧困をなくそう
End poverty in all its forms everywhere
あらゆる場所のあらゆる形態の貧困を終わらせる。

☐ **poverty** [pávərti] 名 「**貧困，貧乏**」
▶poor 形が the poor と冠詞をともなって名詞として使われる場合は「貧困層，貧しい人々」の意味。

☐ **vulnerable** [vʌ́ln(ə)rəb(ə)l] 形 「**傷つきやすい，脆弱な**」 1.3
▶be vulnerable to …「…を受けやすい，…に弱い」。
▶前出の the poor 同様に，冠詞 the をともなって使われるときはそのグループ（脆弱層）を指す。

☐ **property** [prápərti] 名 「**財産**」 1.4
▶価値の有無にかかわらず所有しているものを表す。

☐ **eradication** [ɪrædəkéɪʃ(ə)n] 名 「**撲滅**」 1.b
▶動詞は eradicate「…を撲滅する」。eradicate infectious diseases「感染症を撲滅する」。

飢餓をゼロに
End hunger, achieve food security and improved nutrition and promote sustainable agriculture
飢餓を終わらせ，食料安全保障及び栄養改善を実現し，持続可能な農業を促進する。

☐ **hunger** [hʌ́ŋgər] 名 「**飢餓**」
▶hungry は空腹の状態を表す形容詞。
▶hunger が動詞で使用される場合，for などをともない「熱望する」の意味になる。

☐ **nutrition** [n(j)u:tríʃ(ə)n] 名 「**栄養**」
▶nutritious 形は「栄養のある」（2.1）。

☐ **genetic** [dʒənétik] 形 「**遺伝的な**」 2.5
▶genetically modified organism(GMO)「遺伝子組みかえ生物」。

☐ **diversity** [dɪvə́:rsəti] 名 「**多様性**」 2.5
▶diversified 形「多様化された」。

☐ **cultivate** [kʌ́ltəvèɪt] 動 「**…を栽培する**」 2.5
▶culture「文化」や agriculture「農業」と同じ語源。

すべての人に健康と福祉を
Ensure healthy lives and promote well-being for all at all ages
あらゆる年齢のすべての人々の健康的な生活を確保し，福祉を促進する。

☐ **mortality ratio** [mɔ:rtǽləti réɪʃou] 名 「**死亡率**」 3.1
▶mortal [mɔ́:rt(ə)l] 形「死すべき，死を免れない」。

☐ **epidemic** [epədémɪk] 名 「**(伝染病の)流行**」 3.3
▶pandemic [pændémɪk] は「世界的な大流行」。

☐ **hazardous** [hǽzərdəs] 形 「**有害な**」 3.9
▶「危険な」と訳されることが多い。名詞形は hazard。dangerous よりかたい表現。

質の高い教育をみんなに
Ensure inclusive and equitable quality education and promote lifelong learning opportunities for all
すべての人々への，包摂的かつ公正な質の高い教育を確保し，生涯学習の機会を促進する。

☐ **literacy** [lít(ə)rəsi] 名 「**読み書き能力**」 4.6
▶literacy rate「識字率」。

☐ **numeracy** [n(j)ú:m(ə)rəsi] 名 「**基本的計算能力**」 4.6

ジェンダー平等を実現しよう
Achieve gender equality and empower all women and girls
ジェンダーの平等を達成し，すべての女性と女児のエンパワーメントを図る。

☐ **gender** [dʒéndər] 名 「**ジェンダー**」
▶sex が生物学的な特徴を表すのに対し，gender は男，女，あるいはまったく別の性別として自身が理解している性別を表す。人間以外の生物に gender は使わない。

☐ **discrimination** [dɪskrɪmənéɪʃ(ə)n] 名 「**差別**」 5.1
▶10.3に discriminatory 形「差別的な」もある。

安全な水とトイレを世界中に
Ensure access to water and sanitation for all
すべての人々の水と衛生の利用可能性と持続可能な管理を確保する。

☐ **sanitation** [sænətéɪʃ(ə)n] 名 「**衛生**」
▶似た意味の hygiene [háɪʤiːn] 名「衛生」も6.2 に出てくるが，sanitation が社会全体の清潔さを保つことに対し，hygiene は個人の健康を維持するためのもの。公衆衛生に関して hygiene は使用されない。

エネルギーをみんなにそしてクリーンに
Ensure access to affordable, reliable, sustainable and modern energy
すべての人々の，安価かつ信頼できる持続可能な近代的エネルギーへのアクセスを確保する。

☐ **renewable energy** [rɪn(j)úːəb(ə)l -] 名 「**再生可能エネルギー**」 **7.2**
▶太陽光，水力，風力などの自然の力で補充されるエネルギー。

☐ **fossil fuel** [fás(ə)l -] 名 「**化石燃料**」 **7.a**
▶石炭や石油など，化石となった有機物で燃料に使われてきたもの。エネルギーを取り出した後に排出される二酸化炭素などが環境問題として取り上げられているため，再生可能エネルギーの使用が世界的により注目を浴びている。

働きがいも経済成長も
Promote inclusive and sustainable economic growth, employment and decent work for all
包摂的かつ持続可能な経済成長及びすべての人々の完全かつ生産的な雇用と働きがいのある人間らしい雇用（ディーセント・ワーク）を促進する。

☐ **gross domestic product** 名 「**GDP＝国内総生産**」 **8.1**
▶国内の市場で取引された物やサービスの付加価値の総計。

☐ **child labor** [- léɪbər] 名 「**児童労働**」 **8.7**
▶国際労働機関（ILO）では，就業が認められる最低年齢は15歳以上と規定されている。

☐ **migrant** [máɪɡrənt] 形 「**移住（性の）**」 **8.8**
▶名詞もある。women migrants「女性の移住労働者」。

▶似た単語で immigrant [íməɡrənt] 名「移住者」もあるが，migrant が「仕事やよりよい生活環境を求めてある場所から別の場所に移動する人」に対し，immigrant は「永住する目的で外国から移住してくる人」の意味。

産業と技術革新の基盤をつくろう
Build resilient infrastructure, promote sustainable industrialization and foster innovation
強靱（レジリエント）なインフラ構築，包摂的かつ持続可能な産業化の促進及びイノベーションの推進を図る。

☐ **respective** [rɪspéktɪv] 形 「**能力に応じた**」 **9.4**
▶「それぞれの」と訳されることが多い。同じように「それぞれの」の意味をもつ each と異なり複数形が続く。

☐ **diversification** [dɪvə̀ːrsɪfəkéɪʃ(ə)n] 名 「**多様化**」 **9.b**
▶diversify の名詞形。

人や国の不平等をなくそう
Reduce inequality within and among countries
各国内及び各国間の不平等を是正する

☐ **inequality** [ìnɪkwáləti] 名 「**不平等**」
▶⇔ equality「平等」。

☐ **disability** [dìsəbíləti] 名 「**障害**」 **10.2**
▶動詞は disable [dɪséɪb(ə)l]。disabled「障害のある」。

☐ **wage** [wéɪʤ] 名 「**賃金**」 **10.4**
▶毎月支払われる salary と違い，wage は時間や日にちごとに支払われる。

住み続けられるまちづくりを
Make cities inclusive, safe, resilient and sustainable
包摂的で安全かつ強靱（レジリエント）で持続可能な都市及び人間居住を実現する

☐ **urbanization** [ə̀ːrbənəzéɪʃ(ə)n] 名 「**都市化**」 **11.3**
▶urban [ə́ːrbən] 形「都市の」，urbanize [ə́ːrbənàɪz] 動「…を都市化する」。

☐ **municipal** [mjʊnísəp(ə)l] 形 「**都市の**」 **11.6**
▶（市区町村など）地方自治体の。municipal high school「市立高校」。

つくる責任つかう責任
Ensure sustainable consumption and production patterns
持続可能な生産消費形態を確保する

□ **retail** [ríːtèɪl] 名 「小売」 12.3
▶動詞「…を小売りする」，副詞「小売りで」も同形。

□ **procurement** [prəkjúərmənt] 名 「調達」 12.7
▶動詞は procure「…を調達する」。

気候変動に具体的な対策を
Take urgent action to combat climate change and its impacts
気候変動及びその影響を軽減するための緊急対策を講じる

□ **transparency** [trænspé(ə)rənsi] 名 「透明性」 13.a
▶transparent 形「透明な」。

海の豊かさを守ろう
Conserve and sustainably use the oceans, seas and marine resources
持続可能な開発のために海洋・海洋資源を保全し，持続可能な形で利用する。

□ **the oceans, seas and marine resources** 「海洋・海洋資源」
▶ocean, sea, marine いずれも海を表す語であるが，ocean は「大洋」といった，sea よりも広い海を表す際に使われることが多い。sea はより一般的な「海」を表す語，marine は「海の」を意味する形容詞。

□ **debris** [dəbríː] 名 「ごみ」 14.1
▶「がれき，破片」の意味のフランス語源の語。アクセント位置と語末の発音に注意。

□ **fishery** [fíʃəri] 名 「漁業」 14.6
▶「水産業，漁場」の意味もある。

陸の豊かさも守ろう
Sustainably manage forests, combat desertification, halt and reverse land degradation, halt biodiversity loss
陸域生態系の保護，回復，持続可能な利用の推進，持続可能な森林の経営，砂漠化への対処，ならびに土地の劣化の阻止・回復及び生物多様性の損失を阻止する

□ **desertification** [dɪzəˌrtəfəkéɪʃ(ə)n] 名 「砂漠化」
▶desert [dézərt] 名「砂漠」, desertify [dɪzə́ːrtəfaɪ] 動「…を砂漠化する」。

□ **deforestation** [diːfɔ̀(ː)rɪstéɪʃ(ə)n] 名 「森林伐採」 15.2
▶forestation「造林，植林」に反対の意味の接頭辞 de- が付いた形。

□ **reforestation** [riːfɔ̀ːrɪstéɪʃ(ə)n] 名 「再植林」 15.2
▶「再び」の意味の接頭辞 re- が付いた形。

□ **poaching** [póʊtʃɪŋ] 名 「密猟」 15.7
▶poach 動「…を密猟する」。

□ **trafficking** [træfɪkɪŋ] 名 「(違法な)取引」 15.7
▶traffic は「交通」の意味だが，動詞で使われると「(違法な)取引をする」の意味になることが多い。

平和と公正をすべての人に
Promote just, peaceful and inclusive societies
持続可能な開発のための平和で包摂的な社会を促進し，すべての人々に司法へのアクセスを提供し，あらゆるレベルにおいて効果的で説明責任のある包摂的な制度を構築する。

□ **torture** [tɔ́ːrtʃər] 名 「拷問」 16.2
▶動詞でも使われ「…を苦しめる」。

□ **corruption** [kərʌ́pʃ(ə)n] 名 「汚職」 16.5

□ **bribery** [bráɪb(ə)ri] 名 「贈賄[収賄]行為」 16.5

パートナーシップで目標を達成しよう
Revitalize the global partnership for sustainable development
持続可能な開発のための実施手段を強化し，グローバル・パートナーシップを活性化する。

□ **revenue** [révən(j)ùː] 名 「(国家の)歳入」 17.1

□ **official development assistance** 名 「ODA ＝政府開発援助」 17.2
▶開発途上地域の開発を目的とする政府及び政府関係機関による資金・技術提供などの国際協力活動。

□ **debt** [dét] 名 「債務」 17.4
▶「借金」の意味。発音に注意。

□ **multilateral** [mʌltilǽt(ə)rəl] 形 「(多国間での)多角的な」 17.10

他の教科等に関連する語句特集

他の教科等で学習する内容を，英語を用いて課題解決することで，英語だけでなく，その内容に対する理解が深まります。ここでは，他の教科等で学習する内容を，学習指導要領などからピックアップしました。

国語　Japanese Language

☐ **Chinese character** [tʃàiníːz kǽrəktər] 名 「漢字」
▶common Kanji「常用漢字」。

☐ **classic** [klǽsɪk] 名 「古典」
▶classical Japanese literature とも表される。教科を表す際は classics（複数形）の形で表される。

☐ **colloquial** [kəlóʊkwiəl] 形 「口語の」
▶「話し言葉の」。

☐ **literary** [lítərèri] 形 「文語の」
▶「書き言葉の」。

☐ **context** [kántekst] 名 「文脈」

☐ **metaphor** [métəfɔːr] 名 「比喩」
▶Life is a river.「人生は川のようだ。」のような，別のものに例えた表現。

☐ **euphemistic** [jùːfəmístɪk] 形 「婉曲的」
▶I am between jobs.「失業中だ。」のような，遠まわしな表現。

☐ **rhetoric** [rétərɪk] 名 「修辞」
▶豊かな表現をするための文章表現の総称で，上記 metaphor や euphemistic expression, inversion「倒置法」などが含まれる。

地理歴史　Geography and History

☐ **disaster** [dɪzǽstər] 名 「災害」
▶台風や水害などの natural disaster や，人為的な原因によって起こる火事や事故を指す場合も使用される。an air disaster「航空機の大惨事」。

☐ **hazard map** [hǽzərd mǽp] 名 「ハザードマップ」
▶「災害予想図」。自然災害による被害の軽減や防災対策に使用する目的で，被災想定区域や避難場所・避難経路などの防災関係施設の位置などを表示した地図。

☐ **topography** [təpágrəfi] 名 「地形図」
▶等高線や色を使って高度や土地の形態を表す図。

☐ **modernization** [màdərnəzéɪʃ(ə)n] 名 「近代化」
▶modernize 動「…を近代化する」。

☐ **popularization** [pàpjələrəzéɪʃ(ə)n] 名 「大衆化」
▶popularize 動「…を大衆化する」。

☐ **material** [mətí(ə)riəl] 名 「資料」

公民　Civics

☐ **sovereignty** [sáv(ə)rənti] 名 「主権」
▶sovereignty of the people「国民主権」。

☐ **productive age** [prədʌ́ktɪv -] 名 「生産年齢」
▶生産活動に従事することのできる年齢。一般的に15歳〜64歳を指す。

☐ **voting** [vóʊtɪŋ] 名 「投票」
▶election「選挙」。presidential election「大統領選」。

☐ **contract** [kántrækt] 名 「契約」
▶上記の「投票」など，成人年齢引き下げにともない，18歳から親の同意なくできるようになったことのひとつに，（ローンや携帯電話などの）契約締結がある。

☐ **consumer** [kənsjúːmər] 名 「消費者」
▶consume 動「…を消費する」。

☐ **security** [sɪkjʊ́(ə)rəti] 名 「安全保障」
▶国家の安全保障について言うとき，特に national security と表記する場合もある。

☐ **EEZ** [íːíːzíː] 名 「排他的経済水域」
▶Exclusive Economic Zone の略。
▶領海（territorial sea）の外側，領海の基線から200海里（nautical miles）内で認められる主権的権利を持つ水域。

☐ **employment** [ɪmplɔ́ɪmənt] 名 「雇用」
▶employ 動「…を雇用する」，employer 名「雇用主」，employee 名「従業員」。

数学　Mathematics

☐ **data analysis** [- ənǽlɪsɪs] 名 「データの分析」
▶analysis「分析」。複数形は analyses [ənǽlɪsìːz]。

☐ **formula** [fɔ́ːrmjələ] 名 「公式」
▶the formula for calculating distance「距離を計算する公式」

☐ **equation** [ɪkwéɪʒ(ə)n] 名 「方程式」

☐ **shape** [ʃéɪp] 名 「図形」
▶「図形」全般を表す際は複数形で表される。

□ **function** [fʌ́ŋkʃ(ə)n] 名 「**関数**」
▶「関数」全般を表す際は複数形で表される。

理科　Science

□ **observation** [àbzərvéɪʃ(ə)n] 名 「**観察**」
▶observe 動「…を観察する」。知覚動詞で、ほかにも「…に気づく」「…を述べる」「…を遵守する」などの意味をもつ多義語である。

□ **hypothesis** [haɪpάθəsɪs] 名 「**仮説**」
▶複数形は hypotheses [haɪpάθəsìːz]。

□ **phenomenon** [fɪnάmənὰn] 名 「**現象**」
▶複数形は phenomena [fɪnάmənə]。

□ **particle** [pάːrtɪk(ə)l] 名 「**粒子**」

□ **mass** [mǽs] 名 「**質量**」
▶物質の動きにくさ、慣性の大きさ。質量は地球上でも宇宙空間でも変わらない。単位は kg。

□ **(aqueous) solution** [(éɪkwiəs) səlúːʃ(ə)n] 名 「**水溶液**」
▶saturated aqueous solution「飽和水溶液」。

□ **ecosystem** [íːkoʊsìstəm] 名 「**生態系**」
▶太陽光のエネルギーを源とした、生物とそれらを取り巻く環境がお互いに関わり合う体系。

保健体育　Health and Physical Education

□ **lifelong sport** [láɪflɔ̀ːŋ -] 名 「**生涯スポーツ**」
▶競うことよりも、生涯に渡って健康的な体を維持することを目的としたスポーツ。

□ **first aid** [- éɪd] 名 「**応急手当**」
▶first-aid の形で使用されることもある。
▶形容詞としても使われる。first-aid kit「救急箱」。

□ **cardiopulmonary resuscitation**
[kàrdiəpúlmənəri rɪsʌ̀sɪtéɪʃ(ə)n] 名 「**心肺蘇生法**」
▶cardiopulmonary 形「心肺の」、resuscitation 名「蘇生」。

□ **AED** 名 「**自動体外式除細動器**」
▶Automated External Defibrillator の略。単に Defibrillator と呼ばれることもある。

□ **lifestyle disease** [- dɪzíːz] 名 「**生活習慣病**」
▶病気全般を表す際は複数形で表される。食事や運動、休養、喫煙、飲酒などの生活習慣が深く関与し、それらが発症の要因となる疾患の総称。

家庭　Home Economics

□ **food, clothing and shelter** 名 「**衣食住**」
▶necessities of life を「衣食住」と訳す場合もある。

□ **welfare** [wélfèər] 名 「**福祉**」

□ **consumption** [kənsʌ́mpʃ(ə)n] 名 「**消費**」
▶consumption tax「消費税」。

□ **household** [háʊshòʊld] 名 「**世帯**」

情報　Information

□ **information moral** [- mɔ́ːrəl] 名 「**情報モラル**」

□ **information literacy** [- lít(ə)rəsi] 名 「**情報リテラシー**」
▶セキュリティや倫理的な問題を含む情報の処理能力を指すことが多い。

□ **programming** [próʊɡræmɪŋ] 名 「**プログラミング**」

□ **simulate** [símjəlèɪt] 動 「**…のシミュレーション[模擬実験]をする**」

□ **big data** [- déɪtə] 名 「**ビッグデータ**」
▶全体を把握することが困難な巨大なデータ群。

Sources

Lesson 3

仲谷都，油木田美由紀，山崎勝，Chad　Godfrey『CLIL：英語で考える現代社会／CLIL:　Discuss　the Changing World』成美堂，2021年

Lesson 6

Andrew E. Bennett [Business Sense] 南雲堂

Lesson 14

成蹊大学　2022年度 EPG 方式入学試験問題（一部改変）

Lesson 16

Bruce Allen ／宍戸真　著『Making Connections ／ Health, Welfare, and Environment』成美堂

Lesson 18

Excerpts from *Education UNICEF Country Programme 2019–2023* by UNICEF Cambodia（2019）
https://www.unicef.org/cambodia/reports/education